THE JOY OF HEAVEN 5

Unless The Days Be Shortened

Daniel Leske

."...they shall MOUNT up with wings as eagles..." Isaiah 40:31

Published by: ADVANTAGE BOOKS™
Longwood, Florida, USA
www.advbookstore.com

Library of Congress Catalog Number: 2019955221

First Printing: December 2019
19 20 21 22 23 24 25   10 9 8 7 6 5 4 3 2 1
Printed in the United States of America

Prelude

The"inspired writing continues in book 5. "Unless the Days be Shortened" is from the Bible verse, Matthew 24:22," And except those days should be shortened, there should no flesh be saved: but for the elect's sake those days shall be shortened."

This verse allows Lord God a change in his prophecy of Revelation if he so desires!

It is to protect his own. When I started writing, I thought there was only Joy of Heaven I. Then in time, it became I, 2, and 3. I thought I was done. Then 4 and 5 came about! This is inspired writing and I know one thing and that is the Lord is pushing straight ahead with his prophecy and fulfillment into the millennium.

Book 5 is a step to this and should be read!

As you read the next three books, note that the Creator has the responsibility to govern all the universe as well as heaven.

Earth is very special to the Creator! More special than any of us may realize, so he wants the beauties of his animals, forests, seas, and oceans protected for the future. He sees all of us as caregivers to taking care of the earth.

Read now a book where the Father is drawn or forced into making tough decisions. All of us must bear through these decisions and still try to have a nice life on earth in a time where spiritual battles are on the horizon!

DANIEL

Daniel Leske

List of Characters

Wee Angel:	She has white hair and is always a little smaller than any other angels.
Felicia:	She is about 8 or 9 years old in stature with blonde hair.
Angel Gabriella:	Angel Daniella's identical twin.
Angel Daniella:	Angel Gabriella's are identical twin.
Sir William	(Revelation) A very SPECIAL white winged horse.
Tuddley Teddy	A brown bear that is a friend to everyone.
Jesus:	Commander-in-Chief of the heavenly army.
Paul:	The Apostle, a speaker on earth, now a leader in heaven.
Lord God Almighty	The Creator of heaven and earth.
Job:	A Great Dane with wings.
Quickly:	A beautiful antelope.
Angel Sharron:	Angel guide to mansions.
Angel Joanna:	Angel guide to mansions.
Jeremiah:	A light brown, dark mane and tail, winged horse.
Angel Micah:	One of the power angels.
Annie:	A tall cougar with wings.
Angels, Saints:	The mighty congregation at a special service in God's Holy City.
Friends:	The many friends of Wee Angel and Felicia.(Are you One?)

In book 5, Felicia said, "Look at the glories of God's City!" Felicia and Wee Angel reflect over the journey with Jesus and the power riders on the beautiful white winged horses.

The journey with Felicia riding behind David and Wee Angel riding behind Joshua from the Bible. Book 5 continues as Wee Angel, and Felicia visit more mansions, with more on God's Holy City with a tremendous service where Paul and Jesus speak to the angels and saints. Jesus speaks of Earth, and God's arm with the cup becomes a part of the service, having to do with Earth.

Wee Angel and Felicia continue to meet the Lord's little ones, saints, and others from the Bible. Be a part of this joy of heaven.

Chapter 1

Angel Gabriella, Angel Daniella, Wee Angel and Felicia

They talked about everything. They talked, about the ride with Jesus. They were so in awe. It was a "heavenly awe" Soon with heaven's time, Wee Angel and Felicia knew that Angel Gabriella and Angel Daniella would be going on their way. They knew these two beautiful identical twin angels, who were just a little taller than Wee Angel, and Felicia would be leaving them.

They gave hugs, said their good-days to each other, plus they also hugged Sir William.

Angel Daniella said as they were in the heavenly sky, "We will see you again, Wee Angel and Felicia! We will see you again!"

They flew upwards more, away from the city to another place in heaven. All the riders on the winged horses had left the area. Starbright had gone with the riders. Sir William stood quietly by them. It was hard for them to even think of continuing after all that had happened to them.

They decided to rest and nap by a couple of trees. Sir William laid near them. All of them rested from the long journey, and then after heavenly time, they awoke to a very pleasant surprise.

"Tuddley Teddy!" Felicia cried out! "And there is Annie, Toby, Golden, and Noah with Majestic on his back! You are here. Oh! We are so glad to see you!"

Of course, with the hugs, all of them played a short time. Felicia and Wee Angel sat on their backs. All were happy. They greeted Sir William as well. It was a fun moment for all of them!

Within heaven's time, they walked on the golden path away from God's Holy City. It was time that Wee Angel, Felicia, and Sir William spend some time with Tuddley

Teddy as he didn't have any wings. They walked on the slopes of the hillsides that had more and more trees. Beautiful fir trees were there.

Flowers again were along the golden way, streams, and smaller flowers there too!

Felicia said, "Look at the glories of God's City. They are so beautiful, so much holiness was about them, and the city as it was and always is holy!

Toby was nudging for attention. He liked the attention, and with that, so did Annie. She loved her attention, too, from Wee Angel, Felicia, and Sir William. They continued to walk on the golden path, and they continued to reflect on the journey.

"Wee Angel, the journey was beyond all beyond. I know that I never will get over it. All the angels, all the horses, all the riders, all the light, all the clouds that were on the journey. I'm so in awe on this!" said Felicia.

"So am I!" Wee Angel added. "I am the same as you about everything that happened!"

With that, a couple of saints were close, so they talked again, and soon all walked on their way.

They walked along some rolling hills, with trees and hedges about them. Then an angel flew towards them. The angel's name was Angel Silver. He said that Wee Angel was to take Felicia to a couple more places in heaven. He greeted the animals and soon was off across heaven's lands.

Wee Angel said, "We will walk awhile and then part with the animals, and we will go with Sir William."

With that, they walked on in the joy of heaven. They continued to play with the animals. It seemed with all that happened, the animals and their friendship were more important than ever to them. Wee Angel and Felicia, again took some time and hugged each one.

Both said, "Tuddley, we love you! Sir William, we love you! Annie, we love you! Golden, we love you! Noah, we love you! And you too, Majestic! We love you!"

Then they walked and enjoyed more of heaven.

Chapter 2

The Journey and It's Reflection

As they walked on the golden path, soon two angels and a beautiful gray winged horse approached them. They talked to Angel Abraham and Angel Malachi, and the name of the horse was Jeremiah. He was a lighter brown horse with dark brown mane, tail and he had very bright brown wings.

"What a beautiful horse?" said Felicia. "We know about Jeremiah from the Bible, but that's a beautiful name for a horse."

The two angels said they were to take Jeremiah with them for a time on their journey. Wee Angel and Felicia were so happy with that!

Soon they said their good-days, and they with Sir William and Jeremiah walked again! There were some beautiful tulips by the stream. Some egrets were in the water, some doves flew past them, and the glories were still very strong above God's City.

They still kept reflecting on the beautiful moments they had on the journey with Jesus and the riders. The tremendous praises, singing, and all of the angels gathered along the sides of the valley of clouds.

Then within heaven's time, they knew they should be going on! Wee Angel and Felicia got all their animal friends together, including Majestic for hugs and good days. Tuddley Teddy was more hesitant to let them leave him. He loved it that they could be together, plus Noah and Annie joined in the emotions. They loved to be with Wee Angel and Felicia.

Wee Angel said, "Just know we love you all so much, and we will be getting together again and again!"

Slowly they hugged each again, even Majestic! They spent more time with all the animals, then Wee Angel got on the back of Jeremiah, and Felicia got on Sir William's back. Both of the winged horses opened their mighty wings, and soon they were in the sky. Annie, Noah, and Majestic followed them into the sky, but soon, both knew they were to stay with Tuddley, Toby, and Golden.

The winged horses crossed heaven's mighty beautiful lands, crossed fields of flowers, streams, and flew over and along mountain ranges. Then the two horses flew higher and higher, faster and faster, up and up more!

Soon they flew in just light, which was just below their flight. Within heaven's time, they slowed their flight and flew closer to heaven's lands. Wee Angel said they would soon be at a special grounds for prayer, praise, with mountains all around the area that had high steep slopes.

They started to see these steep-sided mountains with cliff-like slopes.

The two horses flew lower and now above some hills, fruit trees, and other trees of heaven. On both sides of them were more waterfalls. Many waterfalls! Some were high, tall falls and some were very short in height.

They flew lower and lower!

Felicia said, "It looks so special and very quietly majestic!"

The two horses winged onward, lower now, and they flew between some of the steep high cliffs of the mountains. Then ahead, they saw a beautiful open area with many winged horses that waited for the saints who were in prayer at the base of these cliff-like mountains.

A lot of different colors were in the surroundings!

With this, Sir William and Jeremiah landed close by the other horses. The sight to see many winged horses together was something special as Felicia expressed to Wee Angel, "I've seen many times now these beautiful animals and how priceless they are, and as you know, we didn't have any on earth. I know that the people on earth would stop everything to see one of these beautiful heavenly animals and the importance of them for the saints, and angels. I know the enemy of life on earth, doesn't want people ever to know this and all the beauty that is here in heaven."

Wee Angel, "The Lord has always said to us, that he has given the people on earth, the right to choose him. He knew and knows that it is not easy, but with prayer, talking to Him, asking, not always listening to other opinions, but with diligence and

a stand, because it is by belief and faith, they will know this, then he can work with them and guide them."

Felicia answered in agreement and knew what Wee Angel said was right!

Both walked, greeted other saints, played with some of the other horses.

"Felicia, they are always ready to be ridden, walked, or used for flight at any time," said Wee Angel.

Wee Angel and Felicia left Sir William and Jeremiah with a couple of angels who said they would take care of them until they returned from prayer.

Wee Angel said, "We are going to fly ahead along the golden path to another special prayer area in heaven."

All around were high cliffs. They could see many small waterfalls. They flew over saints along the way, and soon they saw the most beautiful prayer setting. They flew over a ridge of hills with the golden path. There in front, in a beautiful valley between the cliffs, were many saints who were in prayer. Along the sides of the cliffs were tall, dark green evergreen trees with huge pine cones on them. The fragrance of these beautiful pines filled the heavenly surroundings.

The sight was awesome as they heard prayers and praise of many saints. They prayed with much on their little heavenly hearts since the ride with Jesus and riders. They talked again about the earth and the decision each had to make to be apart of Lord God Almighty and his creation.

Both knew it was a decision that meant eternity afterlife on earth. They prayed that others would want to make a stand for Jesus, and then they could be a part of this tremendous joy of heaven.

Chapter 3

So Much Has Happened

The open area was vast, yet the sides of the mountains were steep and high. The serenity and holiness were always greater in these prayer areas for the saints and the angels. There were some rows of cedar trees next to the tall pine trees at the bottoms of the cliff-like mountains. On top of the cliffs, there were areas of more tall pine trees.

Vast streams of water flowed out of the cliffs through openness in their sides. There were glass-like rocks all along the streams which flowed close to the sides of the mountains.

Tremendous glories of light went up from the prayer area. Angels hovered up and away from the vast open space. Hedges with flowers were along the base of mountains and around the area. More glories of light, high above, with vine-like flowers, were along the sides of the many waterfalls in the area. The prayer area was encircled on three sides by cliffs in a horseshoe shape.

"Hallelujah," the angels shouted.

Felicia said, "We have been to several prayer areas already, Wee Angel, and everyone has been so special. The angels are here and above, God's glory is here and above, the saints are in prayer, and the angels are always present."

Wee Angel said, "It is just that way here in heaven. EVERYTHING is to praise the Father, as Jesus spoke while on earth, as he is a part of him. Heaven is holy, and these areas are even more holy and blessed."

Felicia continued, "My heart is so stirred again!"

Again some small tears! She thought about these areas and the ride with Jesus and the riders.

"My heart is full!" she said, "Full of this joy of heaven."

Both still walked closer to Sir William and Jeremiah. They gave the horses more attention. They saw some hedges with beautiful mountain flowers, and some azaleas on this slightly hilly area, just to the outside of the prayer area, and along the golden path.

They left Sir William and Jeremiah in an area with grass for grazing along with the other horses. They walked, listened to the saints praising the Lord. The angels were all around, and some had instruments for praising the Lord. They prayed, then quietly looked around at all the gleaming lights that streamed upward and outward from the area.

Soon they were back with the winged horses walking along the golden path. Hearts were full of everything that happened to them. So much to contain, even in heaven.

Felicia hugged Sir William, around the neck. Wee Angel groomed Jeremiah. Both now took some more time to play and groom these two beautiful horses. It was time well spent!

For up the golden road came a couple of saints. Wee Angel saw two more beautiful animals of heaven coming with these saints.

Walking along with the saints was an antelope and another winged dog. This one was a Great Dane. Dave said the winged Great Dane was called Job, and the antelope's name was Quickly. As his name indicates, Quickly could run fast if needed. Job was a beautiful light golden brown dog in color with wings. Dave introduced Keith and Rick to Wee Angel and Felicia.

They talked for a time about the beauty of the area. The animals played with Felicia and Wee Angel while Dave, Keith, and Rick watched them. All three had to take turns getting up and off both Sir William and Jeremiah. They told Wee Angel and Felicia how honored they were to sit on the back of Revelation. All had fellowship and prayed to the Lord. Felicia and Wee Angel looked closely at Keith, for he reminded them of someone they had known on earth.

Wee Angel said to them, "Is it possible that we can take Job and Quickly with us for a while?"

The three agreed, so with the good-days, Dave, Keith, and Rick headed for prayer.

Wee Angel, Felicia, and their friends again were on the golden path to another place in heaven.

Chapter 4

Quickly and it's Biblical

Wee Angel, Felicia, with their little friends, walked along the golden road. They continued to be amazed, and they took more time with their friends. They played, put flowers on, and gave more attention to Sir William and Jeremiah as well!

In heaven's time, they knew they had to fly onward, so they gave some hugs to Quickly. He quietly wanted to go with them.

Felicia said, "We will make sure we see you again."

They wanted Quickly with them, but there was a time when again he had no wings, so they parted with him and bid him good-days. In this short time, they were being drawn more and more to this beautiful antelope called Quickly.

"Just know we love you, Quickly!" called Wee Angel as he stood and watched them fly into the sky.

Job flew along with them, as they circled with the horses waving to Quickly. Then they flew along the edge of the trees and along the lower side of the mountain range to the one side.

They were just above some lilies with a stream, and some egrets were present! They waved to each other, yet went onward on Sir William and Jeremiah! Job flew close behind them.

Then ahead of them were more rolling hills with radiant glories all around them, as saints and angels flew both ways because of the prayer area.

The sight of all the horses with saints and angels was so delightful to Felicia's little heart.

They were still along the mountains, but the area was more open with fields, meadows of flowers, groupings of trees, golden paths everywhere, streams, and a few small waterfalls.

Then, flying towards them was another angel. Her name was Angel Sharron. She told Wee Angel that Lord God had said she should take them to another mansion away from the area.

Then all of them flew now more upwards, higher, and faster to a brilliantly lite archway! It was located between, and in some hills with orchard trees to both sides.

The archway had great glories of light, even more so than the other arches they had traveled through as they went to the mansions.

First, though, Wee Angel said to Angel Sharron that they should take time to eat some of the fruits.

"That sounds good to me!" Felicia said while she was already flying to an apple tree.

Soon they were seated under the apple trees having fresh fruit as the winged horses grazed and rested close by them. There were berry bushes too, so they had some berries as well!

They were so happy and content! Angel Sharron said the animals should stay there, while they flew upwards to another special mansion in heaven.

The grass was always evenly trimmed, as everything was alive and vibrant. The glories from the gateway made everything, even the trees very alive and glowing! It was so bright and brilliant. There were some elk, deer, many birds, and even a few sheep with other animals that heaven had that were not on earth. Beautiful animals, some with wings and some without wings were all about them. Felicia looked at them in awe.

A flock of geese flew by them, and other ducks were in heavenly skies. All were very bright in colors because of the light. This is heaven, and the light is a part of life there. Felicia, Wee Angel, and Angel Sharron ate apples, watched the beautiful animals, and talked about the beautiful sights in heaven.

Daniel Leske

Chapter 5

The Glorious Lights of God's Heaven

They watched the horses and angels in the air. Many groupings of angels flew past them. Some came out from the archway, and others came from another mansion.

Some saints rode horses past them, and they continued to watch some animals in the distance.

Bursts of beautiful light went upward and above heaven's land, which was pleasing to their heavenly eyes. So with heaven's time, Wee Angel said they should be going to a mansion.

They left Sir William, Jeremiah, and Job stay in the area, and soon with Angel Sharron, they walked into the bright light.

Angel Sharron said, "We will be alright for the Lord is with us."

They flew upward and away to another mansion. Onward they flew and flew! They flew more into the very high spaces and through the vastness of heaven in this stream of light. Onward they flew!

Onward they flew! Onward they flew! Onward they flew! Light, and more light, as they flew fairly close to each other but always safe as they traveled to another mansion.

Soon within heaven's time, they approached another place.

They heard shouts of glory to the Father, "Praise to your name! We praise you, Lord Jesus! We praise you! We praise you!"

Soon out of the light, they were on a walkway with still a lot of light around them. Shouts of joy, and then there were more instrumentals of praise!

"Oh! It sounds so beautiful and powerful!" quietly said Felicia to Wee Angel.

Other saints came close to them. They greeted, conversed with them, and then walked away from the light so they could see more of this special place. This walkway was made of beautiful stones.

The views of this mansion were awesome to them.

Up and high above were again these glorious lights of God's heaven. The lights were quietly stunning with the colors of the rainbow. To the sides, up and away, at quite a distance from them were rows and rows of angel singing praises, singing beautiful glories to the Father.

They sang the beautiful language that neither Wee Angel or Felicia understood, but knew it was so sweet to their hearts.

These angels were all dressed in the most elegant gowns with glorious light shinning about them that God created precisely for what they do.

These angels sang and sang, praised, and praised the eternal God of Creation. The heavenly skies were like the inner glory fires of God's heart. There were cloud-like glows over and above all the angels.

Wee Angel said, "Look! Look in the distance!"

Felicia said, "More and more angels!"

Yet all around were beautiful, glowing waters of light in the surroundings. They saw beautiful lights, flowing streams of light, more flowing waters of light above everything and the cloud-like sides, the fire-like light, extremely high up and above the clouds

They walked further away from the intense light of the gateway on a celestial, stone-like path of glories and light under them. As they walked further away, they saw this in all directions.

Angel Sharron said, "This was a mansion of praise and worship by God's holy angels that sing all the time. Glories to the Father! A mansion of angels praising him."

Chapter 6

Angel Sharron
Showing The Creator's Work

As they walked onward from where they were, several saints had been in prayer and praise! They had tears in their eyes as they talked to Wee Angel, Felicia, and Angel Sharron.

She said, "My little ones, these grounds are very special and like the holy of holy grounds of God. Not everyone can come here. God does it that way!"

All of them talked more about the beauties of this place as the angels praised God.

The cloud-like celestial floor of this mansion was of crystal-like gems, hedges of light with little glowing flowers on them. Waters that flowed, but were almost all light, walkways of bright light, yet gem-like in appearance.

"My! Oh my!" Felicia continued to say as she had done before!

Wee Angel, now had a tear or two in her eyes. The holiness was so intense with love and peace.

"Praise to the Father!" They now heard, as every so often, they understood the words because most of the praise was in a language they did not understand!

"It just sounds awesome!" said Felicia. "Thank you, Angel Sharron, for bringing us here! I want to come back here soon, hopefully!"

They prayed together with the saints, lifting up the Lord in prayer and thanksgiving. Soon Angel Sharron said to Felicia and Wee Angel that they should be going to the next place.

They said their good-days to the saints and slowly walked back to the light of the gateway that they came on!" Its light was extremely bright as they looked at it.

Up and around, and above the angel sang glories. Soon they were back in the light, flying and flying! They just flew and enjoyed the unique places of God's heaven.

The light about our three was again awesome and extremely powerful, as they flew in it. Angel Sharron said they had been privileged by God, himself, to the next place that she was going to take them.

She flew closer to Wee Angel and Felicia in this powerful light and said, "Our Father, the Creator, said that I should take you to show some of his work. That's all I can say! Just know the light will get extremely powerful and at times, very bright. We will be alright! Just stay close as we fly!"

Both Wee Angel and Felicia nodded to Angel Sharron. Onward they flew. The light was sometimes very intense even to their little heavenly celestial bodies. They flew and flew in this light, then at times, there were bursts of light to the sides of them as they traveled onward!

Their journey was long, even long by heaven's time. The Lord was with them. The Lord's light guided them. The Creator himself was a part of this journey as Angel Sharron took little Felicia and Wee Angel to a special place.

Chapter 7

Mighty Fires and Light

Then in heavenly time, they flew more and more into the region of God's creation, some of which He was still in the process creating.

They were in light yet saw the darkness of the outer spaces of the heavens, much like Felicia had seen while on earth during the nighttime. They soon were hearing tremendous noise and then extreme quiet.

They saw mighty waves of light and fire, pushing out and away from areas of darkness and void. Some waters were rolling in the darkness, and some were running into the light. Rolling waters along with rolling fires. It seemed like this was a long distance away from them, yet they were close enough to see it happening!

The fires of light, the rolling water, the pushing back of darkness, coming together of grounds, sands, rocks slowly in the forming by the mighty fires and light. They were formed in light, which was overpowering the darkness.

As they flew slower, Angel Sharron said, "The creation continues!"

The Lord was there to see them through the light of the flight, and to show them what he as the Creator was doing!

He said, "I am that I am!"

They saw the waters rolling, and darkness being consumed by light. All his glory present, all his power present! This covered a massive area or region of space, and the noise at times was very, very loud, yet a certain quietness in moments as it happened, both at the same time.

Behind themselves, they saw the stream of light that they had flown in to get there. It still was there as the Lord kept it there so they could fly back in it. They knew that they were very blessed to see this. Rolls of light, rolls of water, that through fires of light, a form happened, yet it didn't happen fast in the creation.

More rolls of fire, light, water, more light, than tremendous bursts of fire and light, power and might! In the heavenly firmaments as God calls them. He is the Creator, he always is creating, that never stops with Him.

Angel Sharron said to Felicia and Wee Angel, "We will fly back in the stream of light. We are in the regions of God's creation being made for us."

They turned and then flew into the stream of light. Then they flew very quickly in this special light that God had provided to another place in heaven.

Chapter 8

Eternity

They continued on their journey as they were again flying in the light to another place of God's. This time they came out of the archway of light unto the shores of a mighty ocean.

They landed on this beautiful shoreline of white crystal-like sands with the ocean close by them. They walked, looked at the beauty, and they saw the vastness of the waters as the Lord had also created these.

Then Angel Sharron said, "We are now going to go again back through the archway of light to another place of God's!"

They walked, and then soon they flew into the glories of light to another place.

This time, they came out of an archway on the topside of some a beautiful mountain range. They walked again away from the arch and looked at the beautiful hills in the distance to the horizon. They saw many mountains below them across the region.

Soon after that, Angel Sharron said, "Felicia, Wee Angel! We will now go to another place."

Back through the archway, they walked, and soon they were back in flight.

They flew onward in this light. This time they came out of the archway on a hillside which overlooked, a mighty region of forests. They saw trees as far as their heavenly eyes could see to the horizon.

Angel Sharron then said, "The Lord had me take you to places in heaven like on earth that showed the vastness of his creation. He created the earth with tremendous beauty. He placed oceans, mountains, and forests there. He placed their lives as he has here in heaven. Keep being thankful, Felicia, and Wee Angel for his mighty creation."

Angel Sharron prayed, "Dear Father, we are thankful for your creation, and we thank you that you have given to earth and us these kinds of beauties. We thank you!"

With this, the three flew in the light back through the archway, and soon they stood on heaven's lands. They were back at the same place that they had left earlier on this journey.

Angel Sharron said, "The beauties of heaven are even greater than earth. Both have life, and God created that life. There are oceans on earth and are oceans in heaven. There are mountains on earth, and there are mountains in heaven. There are forests on earth, and there are forests in heaven. Maybe not the same in how the Creator created them as the earth is terrestrial, and heaven is celestial. Both have life, and the life in heaven is for ETERNITY."

With this, the three prayed and talked about their quick visits. It made a hunger for them to see more and more of God's creation. In their hearts, they saw much that the Creator had done for everyone. They saw his importance. They were more than thankful. They had much love and this beautiful joy of heaven.

Chapter 9

The Winged Horses
are always Special

The winged horses were resting by some beautiful apple trees with lavenders all around the area. Of course, they had been gone for quite a length of time, so they groomed the horses and played with them. Angel Sharron helped them as well, and she took the time to sit on Sir William too!

Then all of them rested by the apple trees as the horses grazed on the grass. They rested for quite some time because they needed rest after the flight.

Angel Sharron had become very close with Felicia and Wee Angel because of where she had taken them. In heaven's time, all prayed together and said good days to Angel Sharron. She gave them many hugs and said, "I will come and see you often! Our friendship is special!"

All of them stood quietly, yet they knew each had to go on, so with this, Angel Sharron flew upwards and away to another place. Both Wee Angel and Felicia kept waving to her as she circled them several times, and soon she flew away on another mission of the Lord's.

So much had happened around Felicia and Wee Angel. They were quiet, serene, yet inside, so much to ponder in their hearts. Soon they walked along the path, leading the horses and friends.

They were delighted to walk for a while and soon were in small hills with trees, tiny waterfalls, and streams that cascaded in and around the trees and made a beautiful heavenly scene.

Little birds, including robins, sparrows, some woodpeckers, and other forest birds, came up to them just like they needed their friendship at this time.

Roses, more lavenders, beautiful glory stones were all around! They came into an area of the forest. There were glory stones along the sides of the streams from the small waterfalls that were located amongst the forest trees. There were special courtyards with golden paths.

As they walked off the golden path, they were at a courtyard that had beautiful gem tables and places to sit for everyone. Some saints were conversing, some praising the Lord. These were beautiful small areas all decorated majestically with these little streams and waters, with lavender, roses, daisies, rhododendrons, and hedges. Birds sang in the trees, which were always glorious, even in heaven!

They also stopped and talked with other saints on horses, angels that had been flying above the golden road.

Wee Angel and Felicia went into a courtyard and sat at a table.

Wee Angel said, "I hope you are enjoying heaven!"

Felicia said, "Wee Angel, it is so special! I keep saying that, and I'm so thankful for everything God is doing for us!"

They looked at Sir William and the others. They reflected again on the journey as Lord God, the Creator, goes onward with His creation and the awesomeness of it.

 A group of singing angels flew along the path, and then they flew up the short path to Wee Angel and Felicia.

Then they sang some songs to them. Good days were said and off they flew again!

"It is so nice and beautiful here." quietly Felicia spoke of the times. "Thank you, Wee Angel. Thank you, Lord, for this joy of heaven."

Both prayed and said to the Lord how much they loved him. In a short time, another angel flew up to them. She said her name was Angel Joanna and that she was to guide them to a couple more mansions.

Wee Angel had seen her many times, so they had much to talk over between themselves.

Soon they were all ready, while Sir William and Jeremiah waited as they prepared for the journey. There was always a special warmth and joy with Sir William in these times.

All of them gave him a big hug around his mane. He looked at them, and they sensed such love coming from Sir William.

"My! He looks so beautiful!" said Felicia.

"He sure does!" agreed Wee Angel, "He is an important, special horse!"

Both looked at how he glowed and said, "Sir William, we love you!"

Heaven is always special.

Chapter 10

The Word and In the Beginning

In time they flew onward in the light. They finally came to another special place.

They stood and looked at the angels in flight. They saw up and away angels, angels, and more angels! All were in the glories. They sang praises to the Father.

They saw glory beams of light that flashed past them. Wee Angel, Felicia, and Angel Joanna stood and watched in awe as the light beams of glory shot past them.

Then to their sides were thousands of lights in a glow yet they were separated by gems. Above the angels in flight to the sides, these beautiful, celestial glowing lights that formed the hills of light.

Above they saw words in flight. A word would be in flight, a thought, another word such as hallelujah, would be in the light stream. Then through the light, all of them viewed a book that they knew was the Bible with all its words. The book was massive in size!

They saw all of this above them with all the angels in flight up and around the word, singing praises and glories to the Father.

They knew they were in a great place of God's heart. They watched all the angels in the beams of light. There were glories, more light beams, the Word, the Bible was huge as Wee Angel, Felicia, and Angel Sharron saw this book in mighty glories of light. Words from the Bible would flow out from it. Beams of light went out and away as far as they could see!

They stood on golden light that was like golden white clouds. They knew the Lord had brought them here to see his Word and to see the flowing of his Word so they would know his power and might! The angels were all in praise. All the glories of light! "Praise to the Father!" They would hear, then, "Praise to our Lord."

Then in time, Angel Joanna said: "It is time for us to leave here."

In a short time, they quietly were back in the light, and their flight was onward as God wanted them to see his Word and the power of his Word. They flew on again in this light.

Chapter 11

The River of Glory

They flew onward, and now they landed on the side of a large mountain, and here they looked out over vast regions of heaven. They saw special heavenly cities of God's! The dwelling areas with beautiful glories above the city. They looked and saw rivers and more glories of heaven.

They talked some, and soon Angel Joanna had Wee Angel and Felicia back into the light, and again, they flew onward.

This time they stood next to and by a mighty river of heaven. They stood by its edges and looked at the other side.

Angel Joanna said, "It's called The River of Glory."

The waters were pure aqua in color. The crystal-like sands with golden glories of light everywhere, that flowed in the same direction as the river. Golden roads came up to and were along the river. They saw in the distance along the river a beautiful forest of trees. They saw bluish mountains along the sides. Then as they looked to the edges of the mountains, they saw more golden light.

They saw beautiful heavenly clouds of glory above the river. It was very wide because they could barely see the other side of the river. The whole region was so golden to their eyes!

Some horses with riders passed close by them.

Wee Angel said, "This is wonderful, Felicia, and Angel Joanna I've been along here before! Thank you, Angel Joanna, for bringing us here."

They talked, and then they prayed, "Thank you, Jesus, that we could visit these beautiful places!"

With this, Angel Joanna had them fly upward into another light stream, and they flew onward in all light. Soon they were back to where they had started from before the journey to special places in heaven.

The Lord had wanted Felicia and Wee Angel to visit quickly a couple more places, including to see his Word in the glories of his heart as he states that He is Spirit, so the Word is a part of his being.

In a short time after they were back, Angel Joanna said, "I have to be going unto another place. Just know I had the greatest time with you, and I will see you again."

With the hugs, she flew away as Felicia and Wee Angel gave more attention to Sir William, Jeremiah, and Job. This beautiful Great Dane with wings flew around and around them with excitement! He liked to have his share of attention, too, as Sir William nodded in agreement to Job.

Many things happened so fast around them. Again they took time for prayer, as they had seen so much of God's power and might in such a short time. They loved heaven, and they loved the Lord.

Chapter 12

Back to the Holy City

Both Wee Angel and Felicia again reflected the journey with Jesus and the riders. They knew who Jesus was, and they loved how kind he was with them. Both Wee Angel and Felicia continued to take in everything around them, and they enjoyed the moment.

They loved everything in heaven and wanted so much to keep going to more places.

Yet at this time, as they sat and talked, an angel came flying to them. His name was Angel Psalms. He told them that Lord God had wanted them to go to his Holy City and see him again. With this, he then said his good-days and was soon in flight above the golden way.

Wee Angel and Felicia continued for some time, then walked to Sir William and Jeremiah. They enjoyed more and more the company of Jeremiah and Job. Within heaven's time, they were up in the heavenly skies flying towards God's City. Onward they flew! Onward they flew! Job flew up close to the winged horses and continued to follow them as he was so happy!

Each one would gaze at the other as they flew over heaven's lands.

Beautiful valleys, beautiful fields of flowers, beautiful hillsides, many golden roads that would go in different directions, streams in all directions, heavenly animals, heavenly birds, were all a part of the journey. Job would even wiggle in flight as he saw other animals in the fields and along the golden way.

Birds, geese, ducks, filled the heavenly skies. A scene of beauty to each one of them. Other saints on horses in the skies went past them or were flying in the distance across the fields. They flew just above the fields. Then, they flew along a range of high hills to their right, with trees, and areas of glories that were along the ridges.

They flew onward! After heaven's time, they started to see glories on the horizon that came from God's City. The glories as they flew got stronger and stronger, which looked so beautiful to Wee Angel and Felicia, because of what had all happened to them.

They flew onward! Soon a couple of angels came flying up alongside them. They nodded to Wee Angel and Felicia, took their place along the sides, and all flew onward!

Then as they continued, a couple more angels flew up and joined in with the group. Onward they flew as the glories got stronger and stronger! Then a couple more angels flew alongside, then a couple of saints on winged horses joined in with the group. Job as he flew, made sure he stayed close to Sir William and Jeremiah.

There was a specialness about Wee Angel and Felicia and all of their friends. They flew, nodded to the others, then waved to the other angels and saints. It was beautiful to Felicia's heart, and Wee Angel felt so special because of everything that had happened to them.

They smiled at each other and at the saints and angels. The group flew over meadows, more fields, with the glories from God's City getting brighter and brighter.

Wee Angel said to Felicia, as she flew up close to her, "Felicia, we will be flying to another gate. I want to keep showing you different gates to God's City."

Wee Angel and Felicia, with so many, were still a little in front of everyone and led the way to God's City. Again, a couple more angels joined in the flight. Then from trees below, a couple more saints riding on winged horses saw the group in flight. Wee Angel watched as the several gray and brown winged horses opened their mighty wings and soon were in flight, headed towards their group.

It was pleasing to see these horses with great strength, open their wings, and fly upwards!

Their group grew, as a couple of angels that were flying along the range of high hills, saw the group, and then they flew to join in the flight.

Onward they flew, closer and closer to God's City. The horizon was bright with the glories of the city and his mighty mountain. Wee Angel and Felicia felt so blessed with all of their friends. Job would always be fairly close to Wee Angel and Felicia in flight.

It was awesome to see how God molded the angels, saints, the animals, the birds, and geese of heaven all together with the specialness of His mighty kingdom. Onward they flew! They saw more hills that got higher ahead of them, and they saw valleys to fly through, as they flew onward to God's City.

Daniel Leske

Chapter 13

Job was Faithful

Onward the group flew to God's Holy City. As they flew, still more angels, saints on winged horses approached and quietly joined into the flight. The group was a pleasant sight as they kept flying across heaven's lands. Wee Angel and Felicia were in the very front with Job.

The hills and valley were increasing in height around them, and soon they were getting higher, yet there was a beautiful valley between the high mountains. This valley led to another gate to God's City. The glories about were so majestic. Again, as they flew, they could not see the top of God's Holy Mountain as it was light and glories above it.

Within heavenly time, the valley widens, with many waterfalls on the mountainsides. At the end of the valley was another beautiful gate to God's Holy City. They flew onwards to an open grazing area along the golden path. Soon they landed one at a time, and shortly the winged horses with saints had all landed there. The angels that flew along with them flew onward through the gate into God's Holy City.

Wee Angel and Felicia smiled and visited with the saints. They expressed their joys for the moment. They talked, and soon the saints left their horses there to graze as they walked onward into the city.

Wee Angel and Felicia took time with their animal friends, gave them attention, and sometimes, even some hugs.

The sides of the mountains were steep here. The gate was still quite a distance yet from them. The glories and colors of light were so peacefully, quietly radiant.

"It's like Holy light around the gate and the sides of God's Holy Mountain!" said Wee Angel. "Even thou the mountain is Holy, with all the types of glory light from this, it is just so quietly Holy for us to enjoy!"

Then Wee Angel said, "We will see you again, Job."

Felicia said, "Now you go on your way. We will see you again!"

Job came up to both of them and put his head by them for attention, so they took a little extra time for this. They left Sir William and Jeremiah with a couple of saints who said they would watch them. Wee Angel and Felicia walked on, smiled, looked about, picked flowers, even a couple of tulips as they walked on the golden path.

They went past some areas of just lilies. Wee Angel said, "Remember Felicia, when I came to you in the field of lilies."

Felicia" said, "I remember very well when we met! We have had some great times already!"

On they walked! Soon they could see the gate in the glories of light.

"My! It looks just like a huge rainbow over the golden road," said Felicia.

"That's what it is! An archway like a huge rainbow" answered Wee Angel.

As they walked closer, they saw the angels up and above, to the sides, singing glories to the Father. The Holy light streamed so that they could only see ahead under the rainbow. The golden road went along a stream, hedges on both sides of the stream.

Once through the gate, then to their left at a distance, was a mountain that was a part of God's Holy Mountain.

Felicia asked, "That mountain looks a lot like Mt Sinai from the earth. Is it like Mt. Sinai?"

"Yes! It is very much like Mt. Sinai, and as you see, the side towards God's Mountain is all in the light as it molds into God's Holy Mountain," answered Wee Angel.

It was so majestic and awed Felicia's and Wee Angel's little heavenly hearts. They looked at this mountain, as an angel flew closer to them. It was Angel Micah!

He said that he would take them to see Lord God. They flew onward above the golden streets of God's City. They had quite a distance to fly, so fly they did!

Felicia looked at everything, as best she could, while in flight. Onward they flew along streams with beautiful waterfalls, dwelling places, open mansions in God's Holy City.

Glories, all around! They flew onward along the base of God's Holy Mountain to a special courtyard.

There were steps and steps of waterfalls, crystal-like dwelling places, high up mansions to the sides, as they flew onward, then upward to see God.

Daniel Leske

Chapter 14

Meeting with Lord God

Both Wee Angel and Felicia went with Angel Micah to see Lord God. The time spent in seeing Him was so blessed and wonderful for us, as it was every time. He, of course, had picked each one up as he had done before and hugged them.

He told them to go to a very special service that was to be held! He bid them good-days and told Angel Micah to take Wee Angel and Felicia to a golden street that went towards the worship service.

Soon they stood, conversed with Angel Micah, and he told them where this special worship would be at for everyone. At that time, he hugged them and flew off on another mission for Lord God.

Both smiled and felt so blessed as they always did after seeing Lord God. Wee Angel said to Felicia, "We will be flying along the golden street to a special sanctuary in God's Holy City at the base of God's Holy Mountain.

They stood and looked upward across the city, seeing the glories of God, angels in flight, saints with wings in flight. All were there! Cloud-like mansions of gems and dwelling places.

They walked on the golden street, and then, they flew onward along the street. They passed streams where the walls of the stream were made of pearls and gems, also specially placed hedges of flowers and vines. Patio areas with walls of gems, beautiful trees, streams with steps to the flow, golden trim on the special stones that made up the floors.

They flew onward! They passed saints and other angels. Soon ahead was this beautiful region or area of glories and light. There were no dwellings places. It was with the city and a part of the city, yet it was an area for this beautiful sanctuary of God's and molded into his Holy Mountain.

As they looked ahead, it was like a cloud of glories that went upward and away from the streets, making a valley in clouds of glory that was the Sanctuary.

Its walls were of gentle, holy light, extremely soft amongst clouds that went upward in the valley of light, soft light that streamed upward!

As they approached, they saw streams of water around the Sanctuary. With the streams of light were waterfalls in God's Holy Mountain. There again were hedges, the most beautiful gems on the edges of the golden streets.

The Sanctuary was walled by light, which came from high up out of the mountain.

Wee Angel said, "Felicia, there are many entrances into the Sanctuary through the light. As they flew closer, they saw an entrance along the golden street. Angels, rainbows of light, smalls steps of water were to the sides. Small walls of gems like hedges were to the side entrance.

The entrance was also light but different from the walls of the Sanctuary. Both stood on the golden street, a short distance from the entrance. Other saints and angels passed them and headed into the worship.

Wee Angel said to Felicia, "Let's pray! Dear Lord, thank you again that you are here. Thank you, Lord, for your time and your hugs. We love you!"

"Me too!" added Felicia.

Again they looked about and enjoyed this joy of heaven.

Daniel Leske

Chapter 15

A Beautiful Sanctuary in God's Holy City

They walked closer to the entrance. As they looked, they could see the golden gems in the archway of the sanctuary. Gems and golds that the light softly radiated through them. There was glorious music being played for everyone.

Wee Angel said, "Felicia, this sanctuary is molded into God's Mountain, but we can't see this because of God's glories. Just know it's molded into his mountain."

Both stood, and soon they heard, "Felicia, Wee Angel, how are you doing?"

Both looked around and knew the voices.

Angel Gabriella and Angel Daniella quickly flew up to them and again some hugs. All of them were together as they were told by Angel Micah to be there.

Soon all four walked through the soft glistening lights of the entrance of light and gems into a vast, vast sanctuary. Once inside, it was so beautifully holy!

They saw a valley of holy light. It was like a valley in hills as we know a valley, but the walls were of very soft holy light. Different from other light. This was holy light.

Wee Angel said, "This soft holy light is for this sanctuary, and there are other sanctuaries around God's Holy Mountain."

So they walked onward through rows and rows of special seats, of select woods and gems with soft light. Many saints and angels were entering this. Soon though, Angel Micah came to them. He said they were to go way to the front, and another angel would show them special seats.

There were many saints and angels in prayer. The awesomeness of the music, singing, and praises were blessing each one as more and more were entering for worship.

Onward they walked and walked. It was a very long way to the front. This sanctuary was vast and very long. So they walked for quite a time until they got to the very front of the seats. There was an angel there that guided them to their seats, which were in the front row and close to where the leader of the worship stood!

They talked quietly and watched as other angels and saints were finding seats.

The seats were molded into the soft light of the walls made with gems. Seats were all around, and seats on the floor of this Valley Sanctuary molded into God's Holy Mountain.

Angels flew and took their places on the high sides. There were thousands and thousands of angels. Saints were on the main floor and lower sides. In front of Wee Angel and Felicia was an enormous platform altar.

"All four were awed by the beauty and holiness around them. They felt so much joy and content to be there. Angels continued to come into the Sanctuary and fill the low and high sides and above! The angels continued to sing and play instruments, while the four viewed everything around them.

The saints and angels along the sides continued to pray and praise the Lord.

Elders started to take their places on the platformed altar.

Wee Angel said as she started to point at them, "Some of them are disciples, Felicia. That is Luke, Mark, who you met, Thomas, Andrew, and James. Now the one sitting over on the side is Moses."

Felicia remembered him leading one of the formations, but still, Felicia kept repeating his name, "Moses!"

Again Felicia said with her hands by her face, "My! Oh, My!"

They quietly took their seats. They were still and quiet and ready for service. More elders came and took their seats.

Angel Gabriella said to Felicia, "That is Isaiah."

"I am blessed! I can't seem to talk. My heart again is so full!"

They continued to sit. Angel Gabriella was next to Felicia on the outside, and Angel Daniella was next to Wee Angel. It seemed to be a special service for not only Wee Angel and Felicia but also Angel Daniella and Angel Gabriella.

Daniel Leske

Chapter 16

A Mighty Special Service

Something special was about to happen. They were a special part of the moment. Now, as the sanctuary was full, within time, angels of praise sang Hallelujahs to the Father. The mighty horns would blow beautiful soft sounds of glory. The angels with instruments played soft songs of praise to the Father.

Now up in the front smaller angels, but bigger than Wee Angel flew to their places. They hovered, and in time, they sang to the instruments of praise with their beautiful high voices.

"Oh, what beautiful voices, they have!" said Felicia to Angel Gabriella.

Hundreds and hundreds of these angels sang glories to the Father. Wee Angel was so thrilled that they were up and around all the sides of this large platformed altar with these mighty elders, disciples, and saints of God on it.

The singing continued while the prayers by the saints along the sides had slowed as they took their places for the service. High above, all around the sides, the sanctuary was now full of angels. By the altar, these little angels hovered and continued to sing praises.

Soon the leader for music and worship stood on the altar and led everyone in singing praises to the Father. Each was so blessed.

Felicia said softly, "I feel something so special is about to happen!"

More horns around the sides blew a mighty sound of praise.

The leader of the worship introduced Paul to speak to everyone. Wee Angel nodded to Felicia as both smiled in knowing Paul would be addressing the congregation. As always, Little Felicia had a couple of tears. Wee Angel seemed to join her in this.

Felicia said, "I've seen so much and now to hear Paul speak to us."

He spoke about Lord God Almighty about the flight of the winged horses and riders with Jesus, and then he also talked about the earth.

He said times are coming to earth and that Lord God Almighty and the elders, including himself, are meeting on this. He left it at that, and He said no more! He said to the elders, angels, and saints present to pray for earth. With this, he nodded to the elders and sat with them.

There was an overall quietness present. It was so quiet because everyone knew of the flight, and what Paul said that Lord God Almighty on the throne is now saying the time is very close.

IT WAS QUIET AND CONTINUED TO BE QUIET!

No angels sang, no instruments played, and all was quiet.

Then as quiet as it was there, the holiness of God was intense and getting stronger with the throne of God so near! The holiness of the Holy Mountain was there at this service.

The quiet holiness continued, then as in through a special doorway or archway into the Sanctuary slowly walked two disciples with JESUS. They were Matthew and John.

All angels, saints, everyone that was seated, stood!

The quietness remained, the stillness remained as everyone was quiet. The power of God was there, with his mighty holiness. They had no idea of what Jesus was going to say! He, as part of the throne, and the trinity would now speak to everyone!

Chapter 17

Jesus Speaks

Jesus, as he walked, now was like the bridegroom and the shepherd, as his gown was long, plain, yet radiant of light. His hair was like the shepherd he is!

Felicia was again in tears as she looked at Jesus.

He walked to where Paul spoke and then nodded to Paul, elders, disciples, and saints.

Everyone remained standing!

Jesus said, "Again, I say! Verily, Verily, I want everyone to know this, whether it be for those on earth, or those here to pray for the earth as I speak these words to earth. It is written in my word:

Blessed are the poor in spirit: for theirs is the kingdom of heaven.

Blessed are they that mourn: for they shall be comforted.

Blessed are the meek: for they shall INHERIT the earth.

Blessed are they which do hunger and thirst after righteousness: for they shall be filled.

Blessed are the merciful: for they shall obtain mercy."

Jesus paused here and stood quietly. He continued to stand quietly after what he had said about mercy. There was great wonder amongst everyone there as they listened. The wonderment amongst the angels, elders, disciples, archangels continued. The Spirit of God was strong in their hearts.

Then it happened, above and through the sanctuary, the arm of God with the cup in his hand appeared before everyone. Then within time, the power of God as his arm, hand, and cup slowly was pulled upward back to the throne. Everyone knew this had to do with Earth and the life there.

Quietness was everywhere!

Within time Jesus spoke on:

"Blessed are the pure in heart: for they shall see God.

Blessed are the peacemakers: for they shall be called the children of God.

Blessed are they which are persecuted for righteousness sake: for theirs is the kingdom of heaven.

Blessed are ye, when men shall revile you, and persecute you, and shall say all manner of evil against you falsely, for my sake.

Rejoice, and be exceedingly glad: for great is your reward in heaven: for so persecuted they the prophets which were before you."

Jesus was quiet again. Jesus concluded and then nodded for all to sit. He nodded to the leader of the riders. The leader had a covered basket next to him. He picked the basket up and brought this to him. Jesus set the basket by his feet.

Jesus said, "Wee Angel, Felicia, Angel Gabriella, and Angel Daniella, please come towards me."

They walked quietly towards Jesus and knelt before him.

Jesus said, "My little ones! You have given me roses, and now I have some for you and your friends."

He opened the basket, and there were many beautiful stemmed roses of different colors. He took out four burgundy colored roses and gave one to each of them. Of course, they were so happy and so blessed, yet tearful as they took the roses.

Jesus said, "You have many friends waiting outside the city gate for you. Angel Micah will take you there. Now you give each one a rose. Also, do a special favor for me."

He took out a larger rose.

He said, "This is for Revelation. He has been so good for you and me. Please put it in his mane. Now thank each one and know I love them as I also love you."

Jesus picked each one up and gave them a special hug.

He said, "Go, my children!"

They carried the basket towards Angel Micah and waited with him.

Now everyone knelt as Jesus walked with Paul and Andrew. He nodded to the elders and saints. Jesus, Paul, and Andrew slowly walked back, and through this entrance of the sanctuary.

Quietness was there because it was as it was! Wee Angel, Felicia, Angel Gabriella, and Angel Daniella remained quiet, too, because of the message as the whole service was still quiet.

Soon the leader led all in prayer, and then the instruments with the angels, soft worship music filled the sanctuary. With this, the saints started to leave the sanctuary. Angel Micah, with the four, began to walk out too! Soon they were outside another beautiful gate to God's Holy City.

A flock of doves flew over them. They reflected and enjoyed the moment. Much was on their little hearts as they stood with Angel Micah.

Daniel Leske

Chapter 18

Back with their Friends

As they stood on the golden path outside the gate, they saw the sky in the distance fill with more doves and pigeons. All in their little flocks as they flew above the hills. Wee Angel and Angel Micah, with the others, flew along the golden path.

Along the bluffs of the hills were cedar trees, many fruit trees, and hedges. There was a beautiful waterfall in the bluff. There by the falls were all their friends. The animals spotted them, and all the excitement began for everyone.

All the wiggling, all the running, and all the hugs that were given between Wee Angel, Felicia, Angel Daniella, and Angel Gabriella to their friends.

Just then, several angels flew towards them from the gate. Right away, Wee Angel said, "It's our angel guides!"

More hugs were given as all the angel guides came: Angel Rebecca, Angel Heather, Angel Joanna, Angel Hannah, Angel Michelle, Angel Sharron, Angel Angelina, and Angel Jennifer.

Angel Angelina said, "Archangel Michael said we should help you."

With this barely said, Archangel Gabriel and Archangel Michael flew up to everyone. Other saints were watching that were coming and going into God's Holy City.

Angel Heather said to Wee Angel, "We will let you put the roses on the animals because we wanted to see all of you too! Go ahead and give the rose to each one."

With this, Wee Angel, Felicia, Angel Daniella, and Angel Gabriella got their friends together. They started with Revelation. Felicia took the larger rose and quietly placed it in his mane up by his ears. He nodded his head, and the look from his eyes was priceless. This time, it was Revelation that had a tear in his eye.

Wee Angel's and Felicia's hearts melted at the sight. The beauty of him was awesome! He was so special that words could not say how they felt about him.

All four flew on and off his back. They hugged him and thanked him.

Wee Angel said, "Jesus said to give you this special red rose for what you have done! We love you, Revelation, and as we knew you, Sir William!"

Next was Tuddley Teddy. He received a beautiful red rose. They put a white rose on Starbright. Then on Toby, it was a burgundy rose, and on Annie, a beautiful pink rose. Then they put on Noah a deep multicolored rose with a nice beautiful yellow red rose for Majestic. Golden received another beautiful lavender purple rose. Zechariah received a deep red rose. Quickly received a yellow rose. Zach and Winta, two of the little winged bears, received red orange roses. Longstreet received a beautiful white rose. Job received a beautiful multicolored rose. Jenna got a beautiful red rose. Jeremiah received a beautiful yellow rose with red trim.

They proceeded and did all the animals.

Then Angel Heather said, "Children, we are going back into God's City.

Archangel Michael and Archangel Gabriel said the same. They said their good days, thanked and hugged each one, the angel guides flew upward just above the golden road back into the city. Archangel Michael and Archangel Gabriel slowly walked along the path back into the city. Other saints watched from a distance, everything that was going on there.

Wee Angel said to the others, "We will start walking along the path and take time along the way to give our friends more attention."

With this, they slowly got everyone together. They were in front with Tuddley Teddy, Revelation, Toby, and Annie close by them. They walked, picked some flowers, looked back at the glories of God's Holy City. They walked on as all their hearts were so stirred to be with their friends.

The glories of God's City was always beautiful! They reflected, talked about everything that had happened to them. They knew special love! They smiled, giggled, laughed as they walked along the way further from the city.

They had plans to play with their friends before they separated again into the lands of heaven. They walked with small hills around them as well as groupings of trees, birds, in a heavenly stream.

Angels were in flight towards God's Holy City. Saints were also on the golden path. They saw saints on winged horses in the heavenly skies.

Wee Angel said, "Angel Gabriella, Angel Daniella, thank you for being special for us! Felicia, thank you too! I still remember coming to meet you in the field of lilies."

With this, Felicia said, "I can't say enough about being a part of heaven. It is my home. I'm so glad to be here. I know it goes on forever! What a beautiful thought. Thank you, Lord God! Thank you, Jesus, and thank you, Holy Spirit!"

With this, all four took time to pray and fellowship! Then they again took all their friends by some evergreen trees with hedges, and a stream. They played with all of them, including Tuddley Teddy, Annie, Toby, and Revelation. They took turns flying up onto the backs of the winged horses. Felicia, Wee Angel, Angel Daniella, and Angel Gabriella loved every minute of this time with their friends.

Then they walked on again on the golden way.

Revelation put his head by them and nudged them with his love. Tuddley put his head by them as they walked on the golden path. Zechariah came up to them and nodded his head. Annie and Toby flew up and around, landed just in front of them, so Quickly also joined in the fun. They were so happy to be together! Winta and Zach, the little winged bears who flew around and around everyone, including Tuddley Teddy, who was enjoying every moment. Job wiggled all over!

Wee Angel, Felicia, Angel Gabriella, and Angel Daniella were so stirred by this.

They walked and praised God!

They had smiles!

They had tears!

They laughed too!

They were thankful, and their hearts were so full with this joy of heaven.

They walked on to see more of heaven.

They stopped, and Wee Angel prayed, "Thank you. Lord, for everyone! We pray for those that have needs. Be with them, Lord. Meet their needs as you have met ours!"

With this, the four gave hugs again to some of their friends. They flew up and over them too!

Then they walked on the golden path. Wee Angel smiled at Felicia. Then each one was smiling. They knew in their hearts such fullness.

They knew the joy of heaven. The joy of heaven was great!

DANIEL

Daniel Leske is available for speaking engagements and public appearances. For more information contact:

Daniel Leske
C/O Advantage Books
P.O. Box 160847
Altamonte Springs, FL 32716

info@ advbooks.com

Daniel has also published *The Joy of Heaven 1, The Joy of Heaven 2, The Joy of Heaven 3*, and *The Joy of Heaven 4* all available from *Advantage Books*

To purchase additional copies of this book or other books published by *Advantage Books* call our order number at:

407-788-3110 (Book Orders Only)

or visit our bookstore website at: www.advbookstore.com

We are planning to have some children's products of the characters from *The Joy of Heaven 1, 2, 3 and 4*. They would be stuffed animal toys, teddy bears, figurines, possibly dolls and other products. For more information:

www.thejoyofheaven.com

Facebook: Daniel Leske / Author

Advantage BOOKS

Longwood, Florida, USA
"we bring dreams to life"™
www.advbookstore.com